Boats and Ships

Chris Oxlade

Heinemann Library
Chicago, Illinois

Designed by Paul Davies
Originated by Ambassador Litho Ltd
Printed in Hong Kong, China

05 04 03 02 01
10 9 8 7 6 5 4 3 2 1

Library of Congress Cataloging-in-Publication Data
Oxlade, Chris.
    Boats and ships / Chris Oxlade.
        p. cm. – (Transportation around the world)
    Includes bibliographical references and index.
    ISBN 1-57572-301-8 (library)
    1. Ships—Juvenile literature. 2. Boats and boating—Juvenile literature. [1. Ships. 2. Boats and boating.] I. Title. II. Series.

VM150 .O95 2000
623.8—dc21
                                                                00-023617

Acknowledgments
The publisher would like to thank the following for permission to reproduce photographs:
Phil Thomas, p. 8; Corbis/Neil Rabinowitz, p. 5; Joel W. Rogers, pp. 6, 9; Dave G. Houser, pp. 14, 16; Carl Purcell, pp. 19, 29; Quadrant Picture Library/Graham Laughton, p. 4; Mike Nicholson, pp. 12, 20, 21; The Stock Market/Tom Stewart, Tony Stone Images/Gordon Fisher, p. 10; Tony Craddock, p. 11; David H. Endersbee, p. 17; Vince Streano, p. 22; Sylvain Grandadam, p. 23; John Lund, p. 24; Ian Murphy, p. 25; Oli Tennent, p. 26; James Bareham, p. 27; Robin Smith, p. 28; Trip/H. Rogers, pp. 7, 18; M. Garrett, p. 15.
Cover photo: Tony Stone

Every effort has been made to contact copyright holders of any material reproduced in this book. Any omissions will be rectified in subsequent printings if notice is given to the publisher.

Note to the Reader

Some words are shown in bold, **like this**.
You can find out what they mean by looking in the glossary.

Contents

What Is a Boat? 4

How Boats Work 6

First Boats 8

Where Are Boats Used? 10

Fishing Boats 12

Gondolas 14

Ferries 16

Hydrofoils 18

Aircraft Carriers 20

Sailing Ships 22

Container Ships 24

Powerboats 26

Ocean Liners 28

Important Dates 30

Glossary 31

More Books to Read 32

Index 32

What Is a Boat?

A boat is a craft that travels on water. People use boats for fishing, traveling, and for fun. Ships are bigger than boats. Ships are mainly used in deep water.

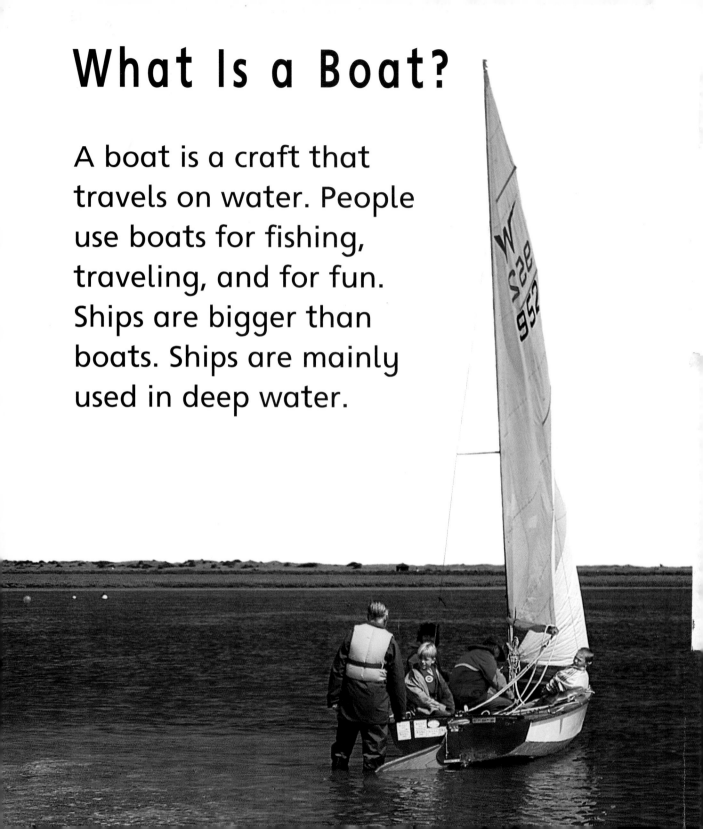

All ships have a **crew** of sailors. They **steer** the ship and work its machinery. The captain is the person in charge of the ship and its crew.

How Boats Work

Some small boats, such as this kayak, move by paddle power. The paddler also uses the paddle to **steer** to the left or right.

rudder   propeller

Larger boats and ships have an **engine** that turns a **propeller**. The propeller pushes the boat through the water. A **rudder** steers the boat to the left or to the right.

7

First Boats

This wooden boat is called a longboat. People called Vikings built boats like this about a thousand years ago. The boats traveled long distances across the ocean.

This steamship was called *Leviathan*. It was built about 150 years ago. Passengers traveled in it across the Atlantic Ocean between Europe and the United States.

Where Are Boats Used?

Ships and large boats travel from one **port** to another across seas and oceans. They often must travel through stormy weather that causes large waves.

Some boats are not used on seas and oceans. They only travel on rivers, lakes, and **canals**. This **barge** is wide and flat to carry lots of **cargo** along a river.

Fishing Boats

Every day, fishers go out to sea in their fishing boats to try to catch fish. Some fishing boats stay at sea for many days or even weeks.

Workers use large nets to catch fish. They throw the nets into the sea. The boat pulls the nets through the water, and fish become trapped in the nets. These men are sorting their catch.

Gondolas

In Venice, Italy, there are **canals** instead of streets. People use boats called gondolas instead of cars and taxis to get around the city.

The person who sails a gondola is called
a gondolier. The gondolier stands up
and uses a very long pole to move and
steer the gondola.

Ferries

A ferry is a ship that carries cars, trucks, buses, and passengers. The vehicles are parked on **decks** inside the ship. Passengers sit on the upper decks.

There is a huge door in the ferry's **bow**. It opens to let vehicles drive on and off the ferry. This type of ferry is called a roll-on–roll-off ferry.

Hydrofoils

A hydrofoil is a very fast type of boat. It is often used to carry passengers. Hydrofoils zoom along with their **hulls** out of the water.

On the bottom of the hydrofoil's hull are small wings called foils. As the hydrofoil speeds up, the foils lift it out of the water.

Aircraft Carriers

An aircraft carrier is a type of ship used by a navy. The ship is like an airport at sea. Planes can take off and land on its huge **deck**.

A **catapult** gives planes a push so they can go fast enough to take off. When the planes land, they are stopped by a strong wire stretched across the deck.

Sailing Ships

A junk is a sailing ship used in China for moving **cargo**. When the wind blows, it pushes on the sails, making the junk move.

sails

mast

bamboo pole

The junk's sails are made of cloth. Bamboo poles sewn to the sails make them stiff. Tall, wooden posts called masts hold up the sails.

Container Ships

Containers are large metal boxes that are filled with **cargo**. A container ship carries hundreds of containers in its **hold** and on its **deck**.

At a **port**, huge cranes load containers onto the ship. The containers arrive at the port on trucks and railway cars.

Powerboats

A powerboat is a small, fast boat used for racing. Powerboats have powerful **engines**. The engines make the boats skim across the water.

When the sea is rough, a powerboat jumps from wave to wave. The **crew** has a very bumpy ride, so they must wear seat belts and crash helmets.

Ocean Liners

An ocean liner is a ship on which people spend their vacations. Ocean liners have restaurants, stores, and swimming pools. Passengers sleep in rooms called cabins.

An ocean liner carries small boats called lifeboats. In an emergency, the passengers and **crew** climb into the lifeboats and are lowered safely to the water.

Important Dates

3500 BCE The Ancient Egyptians build sailing ships with square sails and oars—the first sailing ships.

1000 CE The Viking people of Northern Europe build strong, wooden longboats and make long journeys to fight and trade.

1519 Portuguese explorer Ferdinand Magellan and **crew** set out from Europe, with one of his ships becoming the first ship to sail completely around the world.

1620 Dutchman Cornelis Drebbel builds the world's first submarine.

1808 A boat called the *Clermont* carries passengers along rivers in the United States, becoming the first boat powered by a steam **engine**.

1912 The ocean liner *Titanic* sinks after hitting an iceberg in the Atlantic Ocean. More than 1,500 people lose their lives.

1959 The first hovercraft is tested. It is called the *SR-N1*.

Glossary

barge long, flat boat used to carry cargo

bow front of a boat or ship

canal long ditch filled with water through which boats travel

cargo supplies carried on a ship

catapult machine that quickly pushes airplanes from a ship's deck

crew people who work on a boat or ship

deck flat floor on the top of or inside a boat

engine machine that makes a boat or ship move

hold part of the ship where cargo is stored

hull main part of a boat or ship

oar long stick used to push a boat through water

port place where ships go to load and unload cargo

propeller part of a boat's engine that spins around in the water and moves the boat forward

rudder part of the boat or ship that steers it

steer to guide the direction of the boat or ship

Index

aircraft carrier 20–21

barge 11

canals 11, 14

cargo 11, 22, 24

container ship 24

ferry 16–17

fishing boat 12–13

gondola 14–15

hydrofoil 18–19

junk 22–23

lifeboat 29

longboat 8

ocean liner 28–29

ports 10, 25

powerboat 26–27

propeller 7

rudder 7

sailors 5

sails 22, 23

steamship 9

More Books to Read

Cooper, Jason. *Boats & Ships.* Vero Beach, Fla.: Rourke, 1991.

Rotner, Shelley. *Boats Afloat.* New York: Orchard Books, 1998.

Schaefer, Lola. *Ferries.* Mankato, Minn.: Capstone Press, 1999.